I, Pandora
You, Pandora

Muskaan Ayesha

First Edition Published 2020 by Bob Scott Publishing

www.facebook.com/BobScottPublishing

ISBN: 978-1-952819-02-5

Copyright 2020 Muskaan Ayesha

theauthormuskaan.wordpress.com

"Let me learn the true things, not be diddled and betrayed."

-Sylvia Path.

TO ALL THE PEOPLE WHO WANT TRUTH.

PART ONE:

Love blooms from within. Wrap yourself in the feathers of it.

TIGER-ROAR

To plunge your frail bones,

Into the regurgitation of the stars,

That is love.

To disgorge the bile of taunts,

Into the yellow tinged sink of history,

That is love.

To lap at the milk of chamomiles,

And dunk your fingertips into gardenias,

That is love.

To dismantle your beating drum,

And reassemble the pulp into blossoms,

That is love.

To fill the cracks within your rib-cage,

With thick pieces of oak,

That is love.

To bleed the length of the rattlesnake,

Making an abode in your lungs,

That is love.

To rip out the blades from your throat,

And wipe the blood on cotton clothes of revival,

That is love.

To manipulate your lily-livered soul,

Into tiger-roar strength,

That is love.

The only infinite love there is, is love for oneself.

Every other love is ephemeral.

BRISTLES OF THE MOON

The stars and stones danced in the balcony of my eyes.

Like madmen, they only halted to breathe.

Asteroids kissed my lips,

With the taste of silver and strawberries.

The sun buried itself in my chest,

Warmth erupting outwardly.

Apple blossoms blooming through,

My fingertips.

Bristles of the moon,

That seeps into my cracks.

When nature sings for me,

I find myself a part of it.

When the universe holds my hand,

I realize I am the universe too.

THE OBSEQUIES OF DEATH

I twist the limbs

Of the bluebottles

Sinking their body

Into my body.

I chew the aconites

That crawl upwards;

And spit the poison

Onto the pewter,

Brittle pavement.

I halt the tsunamis

That come my way

With just an outstretch

Of my right palm.

I browbeat my demons

Into shadows of nothing.

An obsequies of

Death.

This is what it

Feels like to fist

Myself in the mouth

For being the enemy,

For being an obstacle

Between my serenity

And I.

DIANA

Diana with grace that blossomed into the fingertips of Mother Nature.

Diana with butterscotch sunbeams embedded in her anima.

Diana with honor in her wolf soul.

Diana with royalty in her veins.

Smile like the wool splinters of sparrow feathers.

Aesthetic visage of soft, snow like gaiety.

Diana, the Princess of the people.

I GRIEVE

I grieve.

I do not grieve like you,

But I grieve.

I grieve in the language of spitfires and cremated tongues.

I grieve with my lips locked onto barbed wire,

And hands between the lungs of Tartarus.

I grieve with basil bodies burning in black, crisp blows.

I grieve with ragged blades,

Kissing the edge of my rib-cage.

I grieve with waterfalls of fireflies glowing iridescent,

And whiskey-bitter blue-emotion's fireworks.

I grieve in murky ponds,

And nauseating hues of green-brown.

I grieve.

I do not grieve like you,

But I grieve.

NIGHT

When I say we aren't the same,

I mean that:

I see tombstones lit like fluorescent light bulbs.

Christmas tree star tops.

Glow in the dark liquid poured onto black paint.

I see an Angel's halo large enough to seep light into the night.

Fireflies finding a place to rest.

A jar of pixie dust scattered.

I see onyx ink in play.

Smudged spider and bat wings.

When I say we aren't the same,

I mean that I see leather cloaks splayed out,

Daisies glaring down.

The breath of a dragon: soot.

And the buttons of flaming huffs.

When I say we aren't the same,

I mean that you just see the sky at night.

You just see,

Some stars and the moon.

O'MALLEY

Bee-sting constellations in her eyes.

The sea that churns at her feet.

The ship that sails on her lips.

Rebellious renegade.

Woman of a man's world.

Grace O'Malley,

Summer-scent of strength.

Nay, not the symbol of red and white nor of green and the rest.

The symbol of the womb!

The womb and lips that give birth and slay.

Grace O'Malley,

Red-haired spirit of a fox.

Wolf-hard odes that she sings.

Fearless like the ocean's winds.

Grace O'Malley,

Gold without her gold.

Captured but free at soul.

Grace O'Malley,

That freed us all from bias beasts.

Savior of a woman's dreams.

MORTAL PAINTING

Strip off your clay clothes,

And grind your bones into a fine white salt.

Look through your shell,

Cloaked in a sandy pink gown.

You will find a foul acidic stench,

Swishing wholeheartedly in your belly.

You will find a bloody mess of ropes and strings,

In blue and red, vines around your flesh.

But hold! Your pupils are locked boxes,

Hiding within them the stars your irises were crafted from.

Your lungs are breathing the scent of musky galaxies.

Your pulse is singing bittersweet melodies.

You are more than human and animal,

More than the planets and sun.

You are the universe itself,

Breathing life into orchids and aconites.

You are not dark nor light.

You are not day or night,

But all.

You are the yin,

You are the yang.

You are a mortal painting of infinite dreams.

WELCOMING FORESTS

We illuminated the entire forest;

Not like stars.

Not like fires.

Not like asteroids.

Not like the moon.

We illuminated the entire forest;

Like torchlights.

And cigarette tips.

And glowsticks.

That broke too much,

And spilled too little.

We enveloped the entire forest with melodies;

Not like cricket chirps.

Not like bird songs.

Not like gushing waterfalls.

Not like winds in waves.

We enveloped the entire forest in melodies:

Like banging bamboo sticks,

On great ringed tree trunks,

And shattering glass bottles,

With shoeless muddy feet:

The sound of chaos.

Yet still, look:

Forests welcome us back.

Knowing an art like ours is,

Not like star filled nights.

Not like sculptures,

But like the metaphor of,

Beautiful destruction.

BEAST FORMATION

They called you shallow and heartless,

But my golden heart fluttered in excitement at the aesthetics beneath your ribcage.

My eyes shone with desire to learn a language created in the spasms of pain you danced within.

Wrapping my veins around your pulse as each day passed.

A naive act that had my entire being convulsing,

In obedience and awe towards you.

You took this as an invitation,

To watch my soul strip to nakedness; I gladly complied.

A moth to a light sat at the lowest step of inferiority,

In comparison to my attraction towards you.

The books never justified the intense pull of Beauty towards the Beast.

Not at all.

But in the rattling hole of universal laws,

Relating to attraction and infatuation,

Resides the least famous art of the devil.

When all fireflies of love die down,

Beauty doesn't crumble and wither away.

Beauty doesn't decay patiently accepting her lost lover.

Beauty doesn't reside amidst the spectrum of agony.

Beauty finds her abode within the four walls of insanity.

Beauty becomes the beast.

And so the cycle goes on,

Through the loopholes of infinity.

Now they call me shallow and heartless,

But his golden heart flutters in excitement,

At the aesthetics beneath my rib-cage.

NEW YEAR

She had her fists clenched around the ash colored moon.

Her battered and bruised knuckles transformed into,

A whitish color as she wrung her fingers around his throat.

He struggled desperately to keep his breaths from running out.

Her eyes flashed a dangerous color of endings.

Her hair embraced in the arms of split ends and roughness.

A foul,

Repulsive stench of the undone,

Heavily coated the atmosphere.

Forcing out all her leftover strength,

She wished the moon a terrible death.

December was certainly a ruthless killer.

She bloomed from the delicate sprouts of,

New beginnings and gasped at the,

Sight of the Moon's lifeless body,

Shriveled from the impact of December's harsh choke.

She gently held the thin piece of silver,

That once used to breathe life into the nights,

And gingerly tapped the edges,

Silently feeding the moon,

The food of resolutions,

And achieved dreams to come.

January was certainly an exotic life giver.

PART TWO:

When spring comes, accept the blossoms of love.

When winter arrives,

Let

The

Sunflowers

Go.

WINE OF HEAVEN

I have relished the wine of heaven,

In the mien of your words.

Like burgeoned fruit from summer gardens:

Ripe and succulent with an aroma of Elysium fields;

And fiery like flickering flames of forest fires,

But calm like the shivering shadows of a bonfire.

A euphonious journey into the grounds of paradise.

With the pleasant touch of hellfire.

A slow swim in an estuary;

And a hasty pivot in a rapidly running waterfall.

Like a floating lamp festival:

A peaceful filament of lucid light within the intimate
gathering of the sky and the moon.

A vivacious ecstasy erupting like a fervent clique of fireworks;

And finding its way into my stomach,

Then escaping through my breaths.

DAMN TO THE UNIVERSE

Damned be the skies if a star is not to be named after you,

And may the sun shatter for not shining upon your luminous visage.

Curse upon the trees which have not shadowed you,

And may all leaves fall for not uttering your name.

The roses in heaven may blossom in abundance,

If your single tear finds its way on a rosebud.

And may the roses that prick your skin painfully wither.

The apple:

A symbol of love for its long life after being plucked;

May shamefully turn away at the prayed length of your smile.

May the rain mourn for not showering calmly on you;

And before a subtle stroke of pain is inflicted upon you by

my sinful self,

May I be destined to the kiss of the reaper.

Thirst

The river quivered.

The water shivered.

Petals from the ocean,

Plucked by the sun,

Wilted in the scorching,

Morning breath of the heat.

Absurd thirst gargled upwards,

From my slender throat,

And clutched at the Pond,

Whose naked body turned,

Away from me in shame of nudity.

My hands remained opened,

In a form of unaccepted prayer.

Empty, void from the kisses of,

The clouds. Pity on the white,

Butterflies of the blue,

That could not paint themselves,

Grey for my withered tongue.

You, my reason of existence,

Have left me with no liquid,

To quench my thirst for love.

SWEET NOVEMBER

Sticky October singing slow melodies; somewhat like melancholy.

Warm night sickening skies,

Silently you crept up on me like sunny days.

Spindling summer like dreams.

Sighs of indecisiveness like sugary nothingness slithering on my lips.

Soft, sand like voice spelling sudden security.

Shivering in smoldering scented embrace.

Sweet, sweet November touches me,

With sticky hums and smothering smiles.

See: sand dunes, sandstones, sand seas,

Erupted into something slippery, something seductive,

Something shimmery when you lit my sober self,

Into an intoxicated, coaxed lover.

CANTALOUPE SOFT

Moonlight spilled in your arms,

Periwinkle blossoms on your tongue.

Sunshine intertwined with your fingers,

Mint leaves around your lips.

Mulberry tinged,

Strawberry flavored,

Blueberry cold:

Your eyes remind me of a warlock's cauldron.

Dandelion touch,

Pewter speech:

Amalgamation of it all.

Cantaloupe soft:

Feather, feather.

You left me in the color heather.

Heathen-blue, numb psyche.

Butterscotch bright;

Yellow yellow.

You're but a ghoulish shadow.

COMPRESSED

Compressed is my color below yours.

Your iridescent yellows: warmth of sunflowers.

Your gold-souled emotions: fluorescence of pearls.

Your shamrock anima: cactus thorny.

Your violet rays of violence: ignorantly perpetual.

Your ocean-foam whites: flavour of frost.

Your cerulean frigidity: whiskey-bitter.

Your tuscan sun desire: blindingly fervent.

And I am porpoise like jet and charcoal.

I am cedar and onyx, umber and ash.

MOONLIGHT AND PERIWINKLE IN MARRIAGE

Paintbrush in the hands of the greatest artist;

Bristles shivering in the silky birth of your hair,

Sun-kissed strands of earth.

Your voice like butterscotch tinged melodies.

Scent like spring days,

Poison of Elysium fields,

Elixir of untamed delight.

Iridescent laugh,

Moonlight and periwinkle in marriage.

Warmth that spurs impossible nostalgia,

Mind like oblivious similarity.

Conversations like maps to gold.

BLACK MAGIC AND PRAYER

You are:

The hum the stars stay up to hear.

The melancholy sound of anklets swooning in the wind.

The roar of bangles aggressively touching each other.

The shattering clatter of clay pots kissing the earth.

Contour of village hills in moonlight spills.

The emerging face at the end of the wheat fields.

You are:

The pale visage of jasmines in the light of the moon.

The clanking of chaos in crude melodies.

The giggles of the infinite chasms of the universe.

The grinding sands of glinting grounds.

The glow of grapes in growth season.

The blinding sight of shadows in slow, droopy alleys.

You are:

The bonding of the mystics with their own souls.

The potion of enchantment and addiction.

The answer to my pleads and result of my determination.

The steel pot holding contradicting substances.

Of two different origins and characteristics,

Like black magic and Prayers intertwined.

SPRING STAR

I grasp in the scent of the pulchritudinous,

Blossoms that bloom from your lungs.

My eyes consume the eccentrics of,

The roses that spring from your throat.

The daisies vined around your fingers dazzle,

Their exquisite beauty.

Jasmines jewelling your rib-cage slightly,

Graze your fragile organs.

Wild flowers embellish your heart,

And send your heartbeat to a spring field.

Sunflowers go into a blazing trance in your blood.

Lavenders lick the base of your neck,

And a musky flower envelopes your lips.

Amidst the blacking night,

You illuminate the atmosphere with your lustre.

My beloved,

You are a spring star in a wintered decade.

TRUE NAKEDNESS

I want to want you in a way too deep.

I want to run my fingers through your mind,

And kiss the interior of your heart.

I want to feel your veins against my palm,

And tangle your arteries between my fingertips.

I want to paint a masterpiece with every crimson red drop within your body,

And write poetry about your irises.

I want to breathe into your lungs,

And watch the rhythmic movement of your diaphragm;

Then imitate that very rhythm.

I want to plunge my hand into your chest,

And play with your heartbeat.

I want to feel your breaths all through your life,

And stop mine when I no longer feel yours.

I want to make love to your soul.

RED TIDES

I hid you beneath,

The floors of my being.

Pleaded that you remain buried.

Begged you to spread below my ribs,

Where you are nothing but a sheet of nutrients,

Where you cannot sow a grave from.

But you do not listen.

You bloom above,

And over my waves.

You spit murky shades,

Into my body.

Dead fish,

Going with the flow.

You blow dead fish,

Into my lungs.

I am the ocean, gasping in the clutch of toxins.

I am the winter flounder struck by the loss of equilibrium,

Jerking,

Spasming.

My arrhythmic breathing,

My shallow tugs for air.

It is but an hour,

Till you,

My red tide,

Send me spiraling out of life.

ANCHOR

When the sun splits and spills in the sink,

And ravens claw and caw,

At the veins in my arms.

When bathtub stoppers plunge into my pulse,

And dustbin bags throttle my lungs.

When I become i;

And shrieking shadows,

Blow ear shattering trumpets in my skull.

When the mirror expands and contracts,

In unfamiliar demonic images,

Of something that's not me,

But still me.

It is then that the glimpse of your smile,

Becomes the rebirth of the sun,

But in a smaller form:

Stars.

A million stars fusing into a luminous anchor.

IN BUCA

Hand in hand we can walk in the nippy winds,

Our fingers as cold as the winter but igniting each other.

Languidly laying a white picnic sheet with golden specks flickered on it,

Like we wish it to be the color of our auras.

Placing the silver flask that contains coffee resembling the zealous color of your eyes,

And strawberries as luscious as your words on the sheet.

In Buca, beneath the statue of Rumi in the subtle touch of sun rays;

I wish to recite for you a poem or two about love.

LOVE ME

Love me,

When the veins in my skull pulsate, throb and fulminate.

When calloused knuckles graze against my sweat smeared forehead.

Love me,

When all hope scatters in a pothole of fading figures,

And bounces right into the pit of nothingness.

Love me,

When the starlight blinds me into oblivion,

And delusional sights prick at my brown eyes.

Love me,

When the lub dub sound of aliveness,

Increases into a pace that matches death's runaway blackness.

Love me,

When I screech and halt at stop signs of self harm,

With road rage and impatience as more crimson floods
await me.

Love me,

When my shell will lack all the requirements to be
"pretty",

But the word will be defined in the blue ink of emotions
on pages jewelled with coffee spills.

Love me,

When my soul will wander into the ocean of looseness,

And silence will be a shiver crafting scream of

dejection,

rejection,

depression.

Love me,

To show me that if I fail to love myself,

your love will fill no void.

Love me,

When I am nothing,

And I will love you for everything.

ANOMALOUS EYES

Enraging oceans of mud,

Clung together by fireworks and perfidious murkiness.

A mongrel of hazelnuts and coco beans.

Enrapturing ground coffee and guile sunlight.

Enticing sands and moon spills.

Asinine concoction of lurid daydreams.

Anomalous eyes of yours intrigues my anima.

A fusion of umber, butterscotch and ash,

Leaving me befuddled.

LOST LOVER

My lover is amongst the breathing galaxies.

My lover is below the dripping moons.

Horror! They say my lover has drifted.

In waves and waters away from me.

Hold! My lover belongs to the waters,

And the waves waltz in his blood.

My "lost lover" is not lost until the drum beat in my chest,

Stops spewing his name in bittersweet rhythms.

Hold the hiccups! O thorny throat,

It is not your lover that remembers you, it is you watering wilted plants.

But still! Wilted plants may wither furthermore,

And dry into blackish crumbling petals;

But it is withered stems and flowers,

That become memory savers in yellow pages.

Look! Use your aimless pupils to look,

At the bare fields and sandy lines.

That grow upon them crops so lush,

And prove that nothingness is the base of the universe.

My lover is not by my left side,

Nor anywhere close to these lungs of mine;

But i breathe him into this body of clay,

And these delusional memories make the base of my soul.

ODE TO MY MUSE

There is a place where you love me,

As I do.

The place is called *the past*.

A past from where hummingbirds sing hymns of you,

And my blossom embellished lungs breathe your scent.

They used to tell me you weren't worth it,

But the sun sang for you, the moon dreamed of you.

Your emotions: like black and white piano keys.

Keys with locks that wouldn't open.

Moods like kaleidoscopes and spiral staircases.

Sometimes, your words contained the white flowers you met me by.

Other times, the bee-like sting from your mouth would scar me.

There is a war I fought, where you were the Glock pointed at my chest,

And I was the child that wanted to go home.

Home,

A place where your arms are my walls,

Your voice is my foundation,

And your hands are my pillars.

People would tell me that I am good with words,

Tangling and untangling syllables,

Manipulating sentences,

But what good are words,

When they couldn't make you stay?

PAPER CROWS

The earth and the sky,

I remember, the paper crows.

Honey flows,

And you sigh.

I tasted the moon,

And the sun;

And you speak.

You speak,

And you say,

"I love you."

And the sea smiles,

At the fire.

I remember,

Sticky hymns,

And long nights.

And I remember,

Your voice:

Your voice,

Like sugar.

PART THREE:

Like the leaves of autumn,

Humanity is

F

A

D

I

N

G

~~Away.~~

WOEBEGONE BRIDE

I've psychoanalyzed the mind of depression,

Come to the conclusion that,

Laying out a constant veil over your mind is probably his
favourite playtime hobby.

The blue-breathed,

Blurred out images on the other side of the veil contract
and relax in a rhythm that strains your eyes.

You become this woebegone bride,

And the blade is your groom.

You consummate your intertwining with the drumbeat of
browbeating palpitations.

You give birth to,

Thoughts that turn to kill you.

Noose after noose locking their lips against your windpipe.

You become one of those who are more afraid of living
than of dying.

The bed detains your collapsing body.

The ceiling stars snicker in chameleon-colors.

Somewhere along the line your Groom goes off to have an

affair with sleeping pills.

He weds her,

brings her to your house and gives you the responsibility to make her feel at home.

You succumb to it.

Always on the cusp of letting your surrender become your tombstone poem.

Your mind becomes a gravesite for suicidal tendencies.

Ghost-kites of smiles that turned to dust.

Dust that loves to sink into your lungs.

Depression's mind sings melodies of sadism,

And you are his favourite victim.

CHILD REFUGEE

Dear God,

It is cruelly cold out here.

The wintry wind wears my skin down.

My hands have become calloused and crispy;

Mother never allowed my hands to go dry.

I am merely a corpse now; almost the same as Father's carcass.

I have forgotten how to add my numbers: one, two, th...

(Mother would be raging if she knew),

I am unaware of what day it is and how many months I've been here.

I am stranded between the past and the future but in some place where the present does not exist.

Father would scold me if I made talk with strange men;

But God, all strange men have taken a liking to my bosom.

My nightmares revolve around two common fears now:

The trepidation of another war,

And the perturbation of being unclad.

I haven't been to school yet but I've learnt how to sew.

I think it is wrong but I earn a pound an hour to buy Mother a new shawl.

That is all for now, God.

Till I learn to worship better,

All I ask for it a blanket and an ugly body.

One to protect me against Winter's kiss;

And the other: to protect my lily.

GUNSHOT

Gunpowder and bomb shells.

Graphic imagery flashing on the curved television screen.

A console glued to my fingertips.

Shoot!

Shoot!

Shoot!

Violence: an entertainment.

Mommy wants me to shut it off,

I'll shut her off.

Sixteen and I want a firearm.

Where's the law?

Load,

Aim,

Shoot!

No such thing as license,

And self defense,

And training.

I've done this a million times.

Aimlessly fingering the trigger,

Sitting on the couch that's become as hollow,

As my brain.

The decision between right and wrong has been sabotaged.

School systems can go to Hades,

Glock in.

Bullet out.

Sixteen and I'm a murderer.

Next an assassin.

Dear, world.

I am the plant,

You've fertilized with the dung of video games,

And murder mysteries.

ODE OF THE DEAD GIRL (HONOR KILLED)

Promise me the universe as a whole.

Make me your home, take me home,

Only to sink your love-ship,

Into the ocean of another woman.

Still, I cry stars.

Flesh of my womb, his cries keep me up.

The baby-sound with goosebump-ache, stolen.

Still, I cry stars.

Make my body a temple,

Of insignificance.

Adorn it with fingers,

That birth paper,

My tongue: a language too ancient to fathom.

Still, I cry stars.

Hail me above the screendoors of knowingness,

Only to make me the woebegone victim of your spider-web plans.

Still, I cry stars.

I fall in love,

More than once.

With a heart that speaks like a monk in seclusion, a mystic in obscurity.

My soul brittle-boned about to split into mountain paths that let him in.

Pigeon-letter the declaration home.

Gone.

I am gone by the hands of a blood-brother.

Born from the womb of the same mother,

But gone.

Still, I cry stars.

DEAR DAISY

Dear Daisy,

I cannot explain,

The abominable,

Hardbitten intentions,

Of the Bee;

But wither away and leave.

He suckles on your nectar,

Bittersweet:

Where you are the sweet,

And he is the caustic bitter,

So wither away at peace.

Then far and far he goes;

Into the deep horizon of oblivion.

He forgets you,

Or perhaps he never remembered you,

So wither away in sleep.

Cover your bosom and eyes.

One so that his like may not come,

And the latter so you won't see him gift,

The honey he made from your flesh to another,

You'll wither away in grief.

Dear Daisy,

I cannot explain,

The abominable,

Hardbitten intentions,

Of the Bee;

But wither away and leave.

DETERMINATION IS DESPAIR

A middle aged man limped,

In his decrepit woolen pants.

I only got a little glimpse,

Of his worn out, rough hands.

The fingers of the scorching sun above,

Clenched around his thick shirt, hellbound.

Like the consuming fires of Tartarus.

It was the only clothes he found.

His thin arms ravaged through the waste bin,

Looking for something to sooth the hunger of his stomach.

Leftovers and dirt sucked at his skin.

He must have been hurting so much.

Then his face lit up with joy.

In his hands lay a piece of bread.

The universe did try to destroy,

His hope but he had an unfathomable strength.

Even though no passerby cared.

The middle aged man found determination in despair.

TWO MOULDS OF FLESH

The air clinks with sounds of gaiety,

But four deceased eyes peak at me.

They look real: alive and animated;

Like two moulds of full flesh,

Skin, bone and emotion.

The carcasses of those alive,

Have began rotting: starting within.

The stench of their withering hearts reek.

The petals of Love have begun wilting.

They fight.

Dissecting disagreements,

Digging for arguments.

The four deceased eyes plea to me;

"Make them stop!" they silently shriek.

A mask of anguish paints their wrinkly faces.

The female: a mother.

She watches her kin rip the vocal cords of each other.

The male: a father.

He clasps a arm around his wife;

"Leave them. They do not learn," he says in woe.

The four deceased eyes leave me.

The living continue their civil wars.

Author Biography

Muskaan Ayesha is an avid reader and passionate writer with the proceeds of one book going towards mental health awareness programs. She bleeds out her emotions and ideas onto paper and transforms them to poetry in an attempt to be able to allow her readers the pleasure of being able to relate to her words. Her books 'Sidereus: belonging to the stars', 'Connoisseur', 'You, through the kaleidoscope', and 'Deathly Aesthete' were all published in 2019. Originally, she began her writing career under the pen name "Known as ash" from which she published her first poetry chapbook 'Fire and Ash: a rebellion against hell.'

She holds literature dear to her and explores several genres that are in the process of being researched and written. She hosts events for spoken poetry at local libraries to encourage the youth to read and write and express their opinions and emotions under the right to freedom of speech.

To know more about Muskaan Ayesha reach out to her with at the email **muskaanayesha15@gmail.com** or find her at the website **theauthormuskaan.wordpress.com**

MORE BOOKS BY THIS AUTHOR:

1. Sidereus: belonging to the stars.

2. Connoisseur.

3. You, through the kaleidoscope.   (Available from Bob Scott Publishing)

4. Deathly Aesthete.

Under the pen name "Known as Ash:"

1. Fire and Ash: A rebellion against hell.

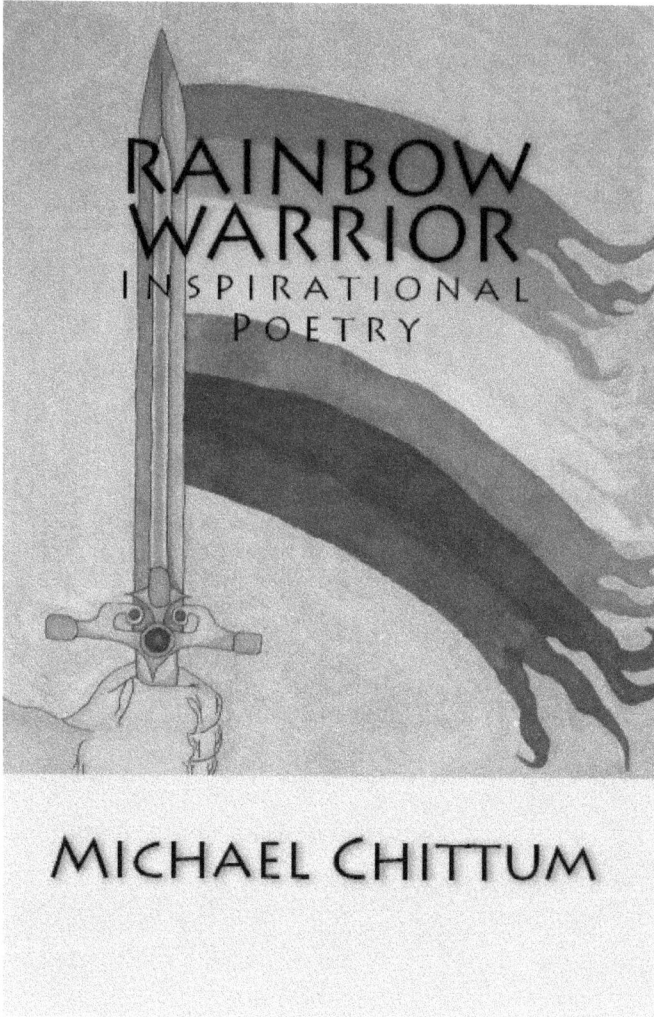

RAINBOW WARRIOR
INSPIRATIONAL
POETRY

MICHAEL CHITTUM

This is a book about the daily struggles of one man. The poems within are heart-breaking, insightful, and powerfully inspirational for anyone who reads them. If you have ever fought to cope with your belief in the Lord, your personal or sexual identity, or addictions of any kind, then reading these poems can give you some answers you need, and the strength to be yourself. If you have ever just wanted to understand these issues better, the insight in these astounding words will stir your awareness. Read snapshots from the life of one man as he strives to deal with pain and heartbreak, bullying and misunderstanding, Faith and addiction. See the man he is, the man he wants to be, and be encouraged by the strength of this survivor, this fighter, this Rainbow Warrior.

www.ingramcontent.com/pod-product-compliance
Lightning Source LLC
Chambersburg PA
CBHW060702030426
42337CB00017B/2719